To

....

From

....

....

Published by
Lion Hudson Limited
Wilkinson House, Jordan Hill Business Park
Banbury Road, Oxford OX2 8DR, England
www.lionhudson.com

ISBN 978 0 7459 7889 5

First edition 2021

Printed and bound in China, September 2020, LH54

The Lion
Easy-read
BIBLE

First Words

Retold by Deborah Lock
Illustrated by Jamie Smith

LION
CHILDREN'S

Contents

Old Testament

New Testament

There are some tricky names in the Bible.
This Bible uses some of them.

Ask an adult to help you say these names.
You will find these names in **bold**.

God   **Goliath**

Noah   **Jonah**

Abraham   **Mary**

Isaac   **Jesus**

Esau   **John**

Jacob   **Holy Spirit**

Joseph

Moses

Joshua

Naomi

Ruth

Boaz

David

There are some tricky place names in the Bible.
This Bible uses a few of them.

Ask an adult to help you say these names.
You will find these names <u>underlined</u>.

Egypt
Jericho
Bethlehem
Jerusalem
Nineveh

The First Days

All was dark, then...

God made light,
and sea and sky and land,
and sun and moon and stars.

God made trees and flowers,
and fish and birds.

God made big and small animals,
and people.
All was very good.
God rested.

The Rainbow

All was not good.
The world was bad.

Noah was good.
God said to **Noah**, "Make an ark."
Animals came to the ark.

Then the rain came.
The ark floated on the water.

The rain stopped and
the water went down.
Noah let the animals out.
God made a rainbow.

The Family

Abraham loved **God**.
God said to **Abraham**,
"Your family will be
as many as the stars."

God gave **Abraham** a son.
Old **Abraham** loved **Isaac.**

Isaac had twin sons,
Esau and **Jacob**.
Esau was born first.
One day he would get all of **Isaac**'s
land.

But **Jacob** dressed up as **Esau**.
Old **Isaac** was tricked
and gave **Jacob** his land.

The Dreamer

Jacob had twelve sons.
Jacob loved **Joseph** best
and gave him a cloak.

Joseph had dreams.
One day, his family
would bow down to him.
His brothers did not like him
and sold him.

Joseph went to <u>Egypt</u>.
The king told **Joseph** about
his dreams.
Joseph said, "There will be
seven years of good crops
and then seven years of bad crops."

The king chose **Joseph** to store
and then share out the food.
His brothers needed food and
bowed down to him.

Saved!

The king of <u>Egypt</u> did not like
God's people.
They had to work as slaves.

Baby boys of **God**'s people
were thrown into the river.
One baby was put into a basket.
The basket floated.

The princess found the baby.
She saved him and
named him **Moses**.

Later, **Moses** led **God**'s people
out of <u>Egypt</u>.
God saved them.

The New Land

God chose **Joshua** to lead the people.
Joshua led them to a new land.

They came to the city of <u>Jericho</u>.
The people marched around
the walls for six days.

On day seven, the people marched
around the walls seven times.
Then they blew trumpets and shouted.

The walls of <u>Jericho</u> fell down.
Joshua led the people into the city.

Sad to Happy

Naomi was sad.
Her husband and two sons had died.

Naomi was going back
to her hometown, <u>Bethlehem</u>.
One of her son's wives was **Ruth**.
Ruth went with her.

Ruth looked after **Naomi**.
She picked grain stalks
from a farmer's field.

The farmer was **Boaz**.
He married **Ruth** and they had a son.
Naomi was happy.

The Brave Boy

David looked after sheep
in <u>Bethlehem</u>.
His older brothers were in the army.

One day, **David** took food
to his brothers.
The army were scared
of a big enemy soldier, **Goliath**.

David knew **God** would help him.
David threw a stone at **Goliath**.
The stone hit **Goliath** and he fell
down.

David was a hero.

Later, **David** became king.

He lived in the city of <u>Jerusalem</u>.

The Big Fish

God sent **Jonah** to the city
of <u>Nineveh</u>.
Jonah had to tell the people
not to be bad.

Jonah did not want to go there.
He ran away on a boat.

God sent a storm.
Jonah was thrown into the sea
and the storm stopped.

God sent a big fish to swallow **Jonah**.
The big fish took **Jonah** to <u>Nineveh</u>.

A Newborn Baby

An angel came to **Mary**.
God chose **Mary** to be
the mother of his Son.

An angel came to **Joseph.**
God chose **Joseph** to take care
of **Mary** and his Son.

Joseph had to go to his hometown, Bethlehem.
Mary went with him.
The town was full of people.

Mary and **Joseph** stayed
with the animals.
Mary's baby was born there.
She named the baby **Jesus**.

Good News

An angel came to shepherds.
The angel said, "Good news.
God's Son has been born."
The sky filled with singing angels.

The shepherds went to <u>Bethlehem</u>.
They found the baby, **Jesus**,
just as the angel had said.

Wise men saw a new star in the sky.
The star showed that a new king
was born.

The wise men went to find **Jesus**.
The star showed them the way.
They gave gifts to **Jesus**.

Get Ready!

Jesus grew up.
He helped **Joseph** make things
from wood.

He learned about **God.**
He heard the stories about
God's people.

Years later, **Jesus** went to see **John.**
"Get ready!" said **John**
to the people.

John dipped **Jesus** in the river.
God's Holy Spirit came down
as a dove.
God said, "This is my Son."

Come with Me

Jesus talked to people.
He told them about **God**.

Many people came to see **Jesus**.
They came to hear what he said.

Jesus chose people to help him –
one, two, three, four, five, six,

seven, eight, nine, ten, eleven, twelve.
"Follow me," **Jesus** said.

Our Father

Jesus told people how to talk with **God.**

"Say: Our Father, your name is holy.

"May your way be done.
Feed and care for us each day.

"We are sorry for the bad things
we have done.
Forgive us.
Help us forgive other people.

"Lead us away from bad things.
Keep us safe.
Amen."

Get Up

A man could not walk.
He lay on a mat.
The mat was lowered down to **Jesus**.

"**God** forgives you. Get up," said
Jesus.
The man could walk.

Be Still

Jesus showed that he had **God**'s power.
He was on a boat.
A storm blew up.

"Be still," **Jesus** said to the storm.
The storm was still.

The Lost Sheep

Jesus told stories about **God**.
"**God** loves you like a shepherd.

"If one sheep is lost,
the shepherd goes to find it.
He is full of joy and has a party."

The Good Man

"Love **God** and love each other,"
said **Jesus**.
"A man went on a trip.
He was robbed and hurt.

"People walked past the man.
They did not stop to help.

"A good man stopped to help.
He took the man to an inn.

"The good man gave money
to help the man get well.
Let us be like the good man,"
said **Jesus**.

Bread and Fish

People liked what **Jesus** said.
They stayed with him all day.

The people needed some food.
A boy gave two fish and
five bits of bread.

Jesus took the bread and fish.
He said thank you to **God**.
The food was shared out.

All the people had food.
There was even some left over.

Here Comes the King

Jesus rode a donkey into
the city of <u>Jerusalem</u>.
The people cheered him
and waved branches.

The people shouted,
"**God** bless the king!"
Some people did not like **Jesus**
being called a king.

The Last Meal

Jesus had a meal
with his twelve followers.
He broke the bread.
"The bread is my body," said **Jesus**.

He took the cup of wine.
"The wine is my blood," said **Jesus**.
"Eat and drink
so you do not forget me."

In the Garden

Jesus went to a garden.
He prayed to **God**,
"I will do as you want."

The people who did not like **Jesus**
sent soldiers.
The soldiers took **Jesus** away
to be put on trial.

A Sad Day

Jesus was put to death on a cross.
He prayed to **God**,
"Father, forgive them."

Jesus died and his body was put
in a tomb.
The tomb had a stone door.
This sad day was Friday.

A New Start

Some women went to the tomb
on Sunday.
The stone door was open.

"**Jesus** is not here," said some angels.
"**God** has raised him to life."

His followers saw **Jesus**.
They touched his hands.
They ate with him.

Jesus said to them,
"Tell other people about **God** and me.
I will send a helper."

The Helper

Then **Jesus** went to be with **God**.
The followers of **Jesus** waited
for the helper.

The followers heard a wind
and saw flames.
God's **Holy Spirit** had come
to help them.

The followers told people about **Jesus**.
"**Jesus** is **God**'s king.
He showed us **God**'s way."

Many people were told
about what **Jesus** said and did.
They followed, too.

For Ever

John wrote to the new followers.
"Live good lives.
Do not give up.

"One day **Jesus** will come back.
We will live with **God** in his holy
city."

When you are ready, why not move on to the next level of reading with **The Lion Easy-read Bible**?

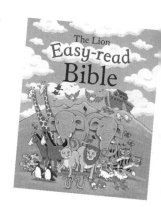